# A Thirst for God

## *Studies on the Lord's Prayer*

# Max Lucado

### *General Editor*

# Contents

# Introduction

There's just something about home—when you're there, it just feels right. And when you're away, you yearn for it. There's a longing for home within each of us. And we all experience a similar sense of longing for our heavenly Father—it's almost a homesickness, a hunger, a thirst for God.

Interestingly, God shares with us that same yearning—that desire is to be our dwelling place, a permanent residence for our hearts.

May this study bring you into a deeper understanding of what it means for God to be the home for your heart. And may your thirst for your Father never be quenched.

—*Max Lucado*

# The Great House of God

> "You are one step away from the house of
> God. Wherever you are. Whatever time it is.
> Whether in the office on Thursday or at soccer
> practice on Saturday, you are only a decision
> away from the presence of your Father ... all
> you need to change is your perception."
> —Max Lucado

1

1. What does it mean to you to be in the presence
of God?

_____

_____

_____

_____

_____

_____

_____

# A Moment with Max

Max shares these insights with us in his book *The Great House of God*.

Remember, this is no house of stone. You won't find it on a map. You won't find it described in a realtor journal.

But you will find it in the Bible. You've seen the blueprint before. You've read the names of the rooms and recited the layout. You're familiar with the design. But chances are you never considered it to be a house plan. You viewed the verses as a prayer.

Indeed they are. The Lord's Prayer. It would be difficult to find someone who hasn't quoted the prayer or read the words. Children memorize it. Parishioners recite it. Students study it . . . but I want to challenge us to do something different. I want us to live in it . . . to view it as the floor plan to our spiritual house. In these verses Christ has provided more than a model for prayer, he has provided a model for living. These words do more than tell us what to say to God; they tell us how to exist with God. These words describe a grand house in which God's children were intended to live . . . with him, forever.

2. What part of the Lord's Prayer means the most to you?

_____

_____

_____

_____

_____

3. How would you describe someone who lives close to God?

_____

_____

_____

_____

_____

# A Message from the Word

[24] The God who made the whole world and everything in it is the Lord of the land and the sky. He does not live in temples built by human hands. [25] This God is the One who gives life, breath, and everything else to people. He does not need any help from them; he has everything he needs. [26] God began by making one person, and from him came all the different people who live everywhere in the world. God decided exactly when and where they must live. [27] God wanted them to look for him and perhaps search all around for him and find him, though he is not far from any of us: [28] 'We live in him. We walk in him. We are in him.' Some of your own poets have said: 'For we are his children.' "

*Acts 17:24-28*

4. How do people reach out to God?

_____

_____  *3*

_____

_____

_____

_____

5. How would you describe God's dwelling place?

_____

_____

_____

_____

_____

_____

6. If God is not far away from us, what causes us to feel so removed from him at times?

_____

_____

_____

_____

_____

## More from the Word

[9] So when you pray, you should pray like this:
    'Our Father in heaven,
        may your name always be kept holy.
[10] May your kingdom come
    and what you want be done,
        here on earth as it is in heaven.
[11] Give us the food we need for each day.
[12] Forgive us for our sins,
    just as we have forgiven those who sinned against us.
[13] And do not cause us to be tempted,
    but save us from the Evil One.'

*Matthew 6:9–13*

7. What phrase of this prayer is particularly meaningful to you today?

_____

_____

_____

_____

_____

8. In what ways does God provide your daily bread?

_____

_____

_____

_____

_____

_____

9. What does this prayer say to you about dwelling in God's presence?

_____

_____

_____

_____

_____

_____

_____

# My Reflections

"You were intended to live in your Father's house. Any place less than his is insufficient. Any place far from his is dangerous. Only the home built for your heart can protect your heart. And your Father wants you to dwell in him. . . . Your Father doesn't just ask you to live *with* him, he asks you to live *in* him."                                    —Max

# Journal

**In what ways do I live outside of God's presence?**

_____

_____

_____

_____

_____

_____

_____

_____

6

_____

_____

_____

_____

_____

_____

_____

_____

# For Further Study

To study more about dwelling in God's presence read Psalm 23:1-6; 27:4-5; 90:1-2; 139:7-12; John 14:23.

# Additional Questions

10. If God's house were a house in your city, what would it look like?

_____

_____

_____

_____

_____

_____

_____

11. What do you think are the significant rooms in the house of God?

_____

_____

_____

_____

_____

_____

**12.** How does prayer give someone access to the dwelling place of God Almighty?

_____

_____

_____

_____

_____

_____

## Additional Thoughts

_____

_____

_____

_____

_____

_____

_____

_____

_____

_____

_____

# The Living Room

*"The first two words of the Lord's Prayer are affluent in significance: "Our Father" reminds us we are welcome in God's house because we have been adopted by the owner. God has adopted you. God sought you, found you, signed the papers and took you home."*
—Max Lucado

1. How has God been like a good father to you?

_____

_____

_____

_____

_____

_____

_____

# A Moment with Max

Can you imagine prospective parents saying, "We'd like to adopt Johnny, but first we want to know a few things. Does he have a house to live in? Does he have money for tuition? Does he have a ride to school every morning and clothes to wear every day? Can he prepare his own meals and mend his own clothes?"

No agency would stand for such talk. Its representative would lift her hand and say, "Wait a minute. You don't understand. You don't adopt Johnny because of what he *has*; you adopt him because of what he *needs*. He needs a home."

The same is true with God. He doesn't adopt us because of what we have. He doesn't give us his name because of our wit or wallet or good attitude. . . . adoption is something we receive, not something we earn.

2. Why do you think God cares so much for you?

_____

_____

12

_____

_____

_____

_____

3. In what ways do you try to work for your "sonship" rather than just accepting your adoption into God's family?

_____

_____

_____

_____

_____

_____

# A Message from the Word

[11] Then Jesus said, "A man had two sons. [12] The younger son said to his father, 'Give me my share of the property.' So the father divided the property between his two sons. [13] Then the younger son gathered up all that was his and traveled far away to another country. There he wasted his money in foolish living. [14] After he had spent everything, a time came when there was no food anywhere in the country, and the son was poor and hungry. [15] So he got a job with one of the citizens there who sent the son into the fields to feed pigs. [16] The son was so hungry that he wanted to eat the pods the pigs were eating, but no one gave him anything. [17] When he realized what he was doing, he thought, 'All of my father's servants have plenty of food. But I am here, almost dying with hunger. [18] I will leave and return to my father and say to him, "Father, I have sinned against God and have done wrong to you. [19] I am no longer worthy to be called your son, but let me be like one of your servants." ' [20] So the son left and went to his father.

"While the son was still a long way off, his father saw him and felt sorry for his son. So the father ran to him and hugged and kissed him. [21] The son said, 'Father, I have sinned against God and have done wrong to you. I am no longer worthy to be called your son.' [22] But the father said to his servants, 'Hurry! Bring the best clothes and put them on him. Also, put a ring on his finger and sandals on his feet. [23] And get our fat calf and kill it so we can have a feast and celebrate. [24] My son was dead, but now he is alive again! He was lost, but now he is found!' So they began to celebrate."

*Luke 15:11-24*

4. When you face a point in your life when you need to return to God, what response do you anticipate from God?

_____

_____

_____

_____

_____

_____

5. What circumstances remind you of God as a father waiting for your return?

_____

_____

_____

_____

_____

_____

6. Why do people expect punishment rather than grace when they think about returning to God?

_____

_____

_____

_____

_____

_____

# More from the Word

[12] So, my brothers and sisters, we must not be ruled by our sinful selves or live the way our sinful selves want. [13] If you use your lives to do the wrong things your sinful selves want, you will die spiritually. But if you use the Spirit's help to stop doing the wrong things you do with your body, you will have true life.

[14] The true children of God are those who let God's Spirit lead them. [15] The Spirit we received does not make us slaves again to fear; it makes us children of God. With that Spirit we cry out, "Father." [16] And the Spirit him-

self joins with our spirits to say we are God's children. [17] If we are God's children, we will receive blessings from God together with Christ. But we must suffer as Christ suffered so that we will have glory as Christ has glory.

*Romans 8:12-17*

7. What is our inheritance as God's children?

_____

_____

_____

_____

_____

8. In what ways do we share our inheritance with Jesus Christ?

_____

_____

*15*

_____

_____

_____

_____

9. As children of God, how do we share in Christ's sufferings?

_____

_____

_____

_____

_____

# My Reflections

"It would be enough if God just cleansed your name, but he does more. He gives you *his* name. It would be enough if God just set you free, but he does more. He takes you home... God adopted you simply because he wanted to. You were in his good will and pleasure. Knowing full well the trouble you would be and the price he would pay, he signed his name next to yours and changed your name to his and took you home. Your *Abba* adopted you and became your father." —Max

# Journal

I need God, my good heavenly father, to . . .

_____

_____

_____

_____

_____

_____

_____

_____

_____

_____

_____

_____

_____

# For Further Study

To study more about our adoption as God's children read Romans 8:37-39; Galatians 4:4-6; Ephesians 1:3-5.

# Additional Questions

10. How does salvation compare with adoption?

_____

_____

18  _____

_____

_____

_____

11. List some advantages of being God's child rather than just his creation.

_____

_____

_____

_____

_____

_____

_____

12. How would your life be different if you didn't belong to God?

_____

_____

_____

_____

_____

_____

## Additional Thoughts

_____

_____

19

_____

_____

_____

_____

_____

_____

_____

_____

_____

_____

_____

_____

20

# The Foundation

*"God is. Not God was. Not God will be. Not God could be or should be, but God is. He is the God of the present tense. And he is the foundation of his own house."—Max Lucado*

21

1. What would be different about your spiritual journey if God only existed in the past tense?

_____

_____

_____

_____

_____

_____

_____

# A Moment with Max

Your achievements, however noble they may be, are not important. Your credentials, as starry as they may be, are of no concern. God is the foundation of this house. The key question in life is not "How strong am I?" but rather "How strong is God?" Focus on his strength, not yours. Occupy yourself with the nature of God, not the size of your biceps.

That's what Moses did. Or at least that's what God told Moses to do. Remember the conversation at the burning bush? The tone was set in the first sentence. "Take off your sandals because you are standing on holy ground" (Exodus 3:5). With these eleven words Moses is enrolled in a class on God. Immediately the roles are defined. God is holy. Approaching him on even a quarter-inch of leather is too pompous. And as we read further, we discover that no time is spent convincing Moses what Moses can do, but much time is spent explaining to Moses what God can do.

The strength of Moses is never considered. No pep talk is given, no pats on the backs are offered. Not one word is spoken to recruit Moses. But many words are used to reveal God. The strength of Moses is not the issue; the strength of God is.

22

2. Why do we tend to focus on our own strength rather than God's?

_____

_____

_____

_____

3. Think of a time when you felt you were standing on holy ground. What was your response to the holiness of that moment?

_____

_____

_____

_____

_____

# A Message from the Word

¹ One day Moses was taking care of Jethro's flock. (Jethro was the priest of Midian and also Moses' father-in-law.) When Moses led the flock to the west side of the desert, he came to Sinai, the mountain of God. ² There the angel of the Lord appeared to him in flames of fire coming out of a bush. Moses saw that the bush was on fire, but it was not burning up. ³ So he said, "I will go closer to this strange thing. How can a bush continue burning without burning up?"

⁴ When the Lord saw Moses was coming to look at the bush, God called to him from the bush, "Moses, Moses!"

And Moses said, "Here I am."

⁵ Then God said, "Do not come any closer. Take off your sandals, because you are standing on holy ground. ⁶ I am the God of your ancestors—the God of Abraham, the God of Isaac, and the God of Jacob." Moses covered his face because he was afraid to look at God.

*Exodus 3:1-6*

4. Moses hid his face out of reverence and fear of God. What do believers do today to show reverence?

_____

_____

_____

_____

5. What have been the "burning bushes" of your life, the things that have caught your attention and directed your focus God-ward?

_____

_____

_____

_____

6. Moses could recognize God as the God of his ancestors. In whose life have you been able to see God?

_____

_____

_____

_____

_____

# More from the Word

[11] But Moses said to God, "I am not a great man! How can I go to the king and lead the Israelites out of Egypt?"

[12] God said, "I will be with you. This will be the proof that I am sending you: After you lead the people out of Egypt, all of you will worship me on this mountain."

[13] Moses said to God, "When I go to the Israelites, I will say to them, 'The God of your fathers sent me to you.' What if the people say, 'What is his name?' What should I tell them?"

[14] Then God said to Moses, "I AM WHO I AM. When you go to the people of Israel, tell them, 'I AM sent me to you.' "

*Exodus 3:11-14*

7. What is the significance of God's name being "I AM"?

_____

_____

_____

_____

_____

8. In what ways do believers represent God to the world as "I AM"?

_____

_____

_____

_____

_____

_____

9. What are some different ways that God meets people according to their needs and circumstances?

_____

_____

_____

_____

_____

_____

# My Reflections

"You aren't . . . the mortar within the foundation; God is. I know you know that in your head, but do you know that in your heart? Would you like to?

"When you are confused about the future, go to your *Jehovah-raah*, your caring shepherd. When you are anxious about provision, talk to *Jehovah-jireh*, the Lord who provides. Are your challenges too great? Seek the help of *Jehovah-shalom*, the Lord is peace. Is your body sick? Are your emotions weak? *Jehovah-rophe*, the Lord who heals you, will see you now.

"God is the shepherd who guides, the Lord who provides, the voice who brings peace in the storm . . . And most of all, he . . . is." —Max

# Journal

**What have I been trying to do in my own strength rather than in God's?**

_____

_____

_____

_____

_____

_____

_____

26

_____

_____

_____

_____

_____

_____

_____

_____

_____

_____

_____

# For Further Study

To study more about God's greatness read Exodus 15; Deuteronomy 32:3-4; Psalm 23; 27:1-4; 99.

# Additional Questions

10. How does God wear different "hats" in your life, like the different names by which he is known?

_____

_____

_____

_____

_____

_____

11. What kind of faulty mortar is mistaken for God's mortar in life's foundation?

_____

_____

_____

_____

_____

_____

**12.** How does the fact that God *is*, make the world a different place?

_____

_____

_____

_____

_____

_____

## Additional Thoughts

_____

_____

_____

_____

_____

_____

_____

_____

_____

_____

_____

_____

_____

# The Observatory

*"I attended church with the son of the mayor. In Andrews, Texas, that's not much to boast about. Nevertheless the kid had clout that most of us didn't. 'My father has an office at the courthouse,' he could claim. "Guess what you can claim? 'My Father rules the universe.' "*
                    —Max Lucado

1. What part of nature reminds you most of God as "ruler of the universe"?

_____

_____

_____

_____

_____

_____

_____

_____

# A Moment with Max

Max shares these insights with us in his book *The Great House of God*.

Nature is God's workshop. The sky is his resumé. The universe is his calling card. You want to know who God is? See what he has done. You want to know his power? Take a look at his creation. Curious about his strength? Pay a visit to his home address: 1 Billion Starry Sky Avenue. Want to know his size? Step out into the night and stare at starlight emitted one million years ago and then read 2 Chronicles 2:6, "No one can really build a house for our God. Not even the highest of heavens can hold him."

He is untainted by the atmosphere of sin, unbridled by the time line of history, unhindered by the weariness of the body.

What controls you doesn't control him. What troubles you doesn't trouble him. What fatigues you doesn't fatigue him. Is an eagle disturbed by traffic? No, he rises above it. Is the whale perturbed by a hurricane? Of course not, he plunges beneath it. Is the lion flustered by the mouse standing directly in his way? No, he steps over it. How much more is God able to soar above, plunge beneath, and step over the troubles of the earth!

2. How does God's perspective as Creator differ from our perspective as his creations?

_____

_____

_____

_____

_____

3. What does creation teach you about the power of God?

_____

_____

_____

_____

_____

# A Message from the Word

[1] Then the Lord answered Job from the storm. He said:
[2] "Who is this that makes my purpose unclear
   by saying things that are not true?
[3] Be strong like a man!
   I will ask you questions,
      and you must answer me.
[4] Where were you when I made the earth's foundation?
   Tell me, if you understand.
[5] Who marked off how big it should be?
   Surely you know!
      Who stretched a ruler across it?
[6] What were the earth's foundations set on,
   or who put its cornerstone in place
[7] while the morning stars sang together
   and all the angels shouted with joy?
[8] "Who shut the doors to keep the sea in
   when it broke through and was born,
[9] when I made the clouds like a coat for the sea
   and wrapped it in dark clouds,
[10] when I put limits on the sea
   and put its doors and bars in place,
[11] when I said to the sea, 'You may come this far, but no farther;
   this is where your proud waves must stop'?
[12] "Have you ever ordered the morning to begin,
   or shown the dawn where its place was
[13] in order to take hold of the earth by its edges
   and shake evil people out of it?
[14] At dawn the earth changes like clay being pressed by a seal;
   the hills and valleys stand out like folds in a coat.

*Job 38:1–14*

4. In this passage God uses creation as evidence of his credibility. Which parts of creation most convince you of God's credibility?

_____

_____

_____

_____

_____

5. In what way does God's creation of the world give you reason to trust in him?

_____

_____

_____

_____

_____

6. How do the heavens tell of God's glory?

_____

_____

_____

_____

_____

# More from the Word

[1] The heavens tell the glory of God,
   and the skies announce what his hands have made.
[2] Day after day they tell the story;
   night after night they tell it again.
[3] They have no speech or words;
   they have no voice to be heard.
[4] But their message goes out through all the world;

their words go everywhere on earth.
    The sky is like a home for the sun.
⁵ The sun comes out like a bridegroom from his bedroom.
    It rejoices like an athlete eager to run a race.
⁶ The sun rises at one end of the sky
    and follows its path to the other end.
        Nothing hides from its heat.

*Psalm 19:1-6*

7. What does a sunrise tell you about God?

_____

_____

_____

_____

_____

8. What part of nature most renews your connection to God?

_____

_____

_____

_____

_____

9. What convinces you that the God who is great enough to create the world cares about you as an individual?

_____

_____

_____

_____

_____

# My Reflections

"If he is able to place the stars in their sockets and suspend the sky like a curtain, do you think it remotely possible that God is able to guide your life? If your God is mighty enough to ignite the sun, could it be that he is mighty enough to light your path? If he cares enough about the planet Saturn to give it rings or Venus to make it sparkle, is there an outside chance that he cares enough about you to meet your needs?" —Max

# Journal

I see God around me when I see . . .

_____

_____

_____

_____

_____

_____

_____

_____

_____

_____

_____

_____

# For Further Study

To study more about God's revelation within creation read Genesis 1—3; Psalm 19:1-4; 139; Matthew 6:25-30.

# Additional Questions

10. What is the biggest mystery of creation?

_____

_____

_____

_____

_____

_____

_____

11. What is the most beautiful natural sight you've ever seen?

_____

_____

_____

_____

_____

12. What question would you like to ask God about why he created something the way he did?

_____

_____

_____

_____

_____

_____

## Additional Thoughts

_____

_____

_____

_____

_____

_____

_____

_____

_____

_____

_____

_____

# The Chapel

*"There are times when to speak is to violate the moment ... when silence represents the highest respect. The word for such times is reverence. The prayer for such times is "Hallowed be thy name." And the place for this prayer is the chapel." —Max Lucado*

41

1. Have you ever had a significant time of silence? Explain what happened.

_____

_____

_____

_____

_____

_____

_____

_____

# A Moment with Max

Max shares these insights with us in his book *The Great House of God*.

We enter the chapel and beseech, "Be hallowed, Lord." Do whatever it takes to be holy in my life. Take your rightful place on the throne. Exalt yourself. Magnify yourself. Glorify yourself. You be Lord, and I'll be quiet.

The word "hallowed" comes from the word "holy," and the word "holy" means "to separate." The ancestry of the term can be traced back to an ancient word which means "to cut." To be holy, then, is to be a cut above the norm, superior, extraordinary. Remember what we learned in the observatory? The Holy One dwells on a different level from the rest of us. What frightens us does not frighten him. What troubles us does not trouble him.

I've puttered around in a bass boat enough to know the secret for finding land in a storm . . . You set your sights on an object unaffected by the wind—a light on the shore—and go straight toward it.

By seeking God in the chapel, you do the same. When you set your sights on our God, you focus on one "a cut above" any storm life may bring.

2. In what ways can believers show God that he is hallowed or holy to us?

_____

_____

_____

_____

_____

3. How does God's holiness help us find our way in a storm?

_____

_____

_____

_____

_____

# A Message from the Word

[1] God is our protection and our strength.
He always helps in times of trouble.
[2] So we will not be afraid even if the earth shakes,
or the mountains fall into the sea,
[3] even if the oceans roar and foam,
or the mountains shake at the raging sea. *Selah*
[4] There is a river that brings joy to the city of God,
the holy place where God Most High lives.
[5] God is in that city, and so it will not be shaken.
God will help her at dawn.
[6] Nations tremble and kingdoms shake.
God shouts and the earth crumbles.
[7] The Lord All-Powerful is with us;
the God of Jacob is our defender. *Selah*
[8] Come and see what the Lord has done,
the amazing things he has done on the earth.
[9] He stops wars everywhere on the earth.
He breaks all bows and spears
and burns up the chariots with fire.
[10] God says, "Be quiet and know that I am God.
I will be supreme over all the nations;
I will be supreme in the earth."

*Psalm 46:1-10*

43

4. How important is a person's *stillness* in recognizing God's holiness?

_____

_____

_____

_____

_____

5. In what ways is God's holiness a refuge?

_____

_____

_____

_____

6. How does God's holiness affect a person's service for him?

_____

_____

_____

_____

# More from the Word

¹ The Lord is king.
    Let the peoples shake with fear.
  He sits between the gold creatures with wings.
    Let the earth shake.
² The Lord in Jerusalem is great;
    he is supreme over all the peoples.
³ Let them praise your name;
    it is great, holy and to be feared.
⁴ The King is powerful and loves justice.
    Lord, you made things fair;
  you have done what is fair and right
    for the people of Jacob.
⁵ Praise the Lord our God,
    and worship at the Temple, his footstool.
  He is holy.

*Psalm 99:1-5*

7. What does it mean to you that God reigns over everything?

_____

_____

_____

_____

_____

8. How can someone *exalt* God?

_____

_____

_____

_____

_____

9. What are some bi-products of taking time to recognize God's holiness?

_____

_____

_____

_____

_____

# My Reflections

"Linger often in the chapel. In the midst of your daily storms, make it a point to be still and set your sights on him. Let God be God. Let him bathe you in his glory so that both your breath and your troubles are sucked from your soul. Be still. Be quiet. Be open and willing. Then you will know that God is God, and you can't help but confess, 'Hallowed be thy name.' "

—Max

# Journal

**God, I know you are the one Holy God because . . .**

# For Further Study

To study more about God's holiness read Leviticus 19:1-18; Psalm 29; 96; 1 Peter 1:13-16.

# Additional Questions

10. Think of someone whom you consider holy. What is that person like?

_____

_____

_____

_____

_____

_____

11. What elements of your life hinder your quiet moments in the chapel of God's holiness?

_____

_____

_____

_____

_____

_____

**12. How should God's holiness affect your behavior?**

_____

_____

_____

_____

_____

_____

## Additional Thoughts

_____

_____

49

_____

_____

_____

_____

_____

_____

_____

_____

_____

_____

_____

_____

# The Study

*"God has a plan and that plan is good. Our question is, how do I access it?" —Max Lucado*

1. Think of a decision you have struggled over. What feelings were involved in trying to make the "right" decision?

_____

_____

_____

_____

_____

_____

_____

# A Moment with Max

Max shares these insights with us in his book *The Great House of God.*

Just down the hall from the chapel is a room uncluttered by televisions, stereos, and e-mail-infected computers. Envision a study with bookshelves lining the walls, a braided rug on the floor and an inviting fire in the hearth. In front of the fire are two high, wingback chairs, one for you and one for your Father. Your seat is empty, and your Father motions for you to join him. Come and sit and ask him whatever is on your heart. No question is too small, no riddle too simple. He has all the time in the world. Come and seek the will of God.

To pray, "Thy will be done" is to seek the heart of God. The word "will" means "strong desire." The Study is where we learn what God desires. What is his heart? His passion? He wants you to know it.

Shall God hide from us what he is going to do? Apparently not, for he has gone to great lengths to reveal his will to us. Could he have done more than send his Son to lead us? Could he have done more than give his word to teach us? Could he have done more than orchestrate events to awaken us? Could he have done more than send his Holy Spirit to counsel us?

52

2. When did God reveal his will to you in a specific way?

_____

_____

_____

_____

_____

3. Why does God's will sometimes seem hidden?

_____

_____

_____

_____

_____

# A Message from the Word

²⁶ Also, the Spirit helps us with our weakness. We do not know how to pray as we should. But the Spirit himself speaks to God for us, even begs God for us with deep feelings that words cannot explain. ²⁷ God can see what is in people's hearts. And he knows what is in the mind of the Spirit, because the Spirit speaks to God for his people in the way God wants.

²⁸ We know that in everything God works for the good of those who love him. They are the people he called, because that was his plan. ²⁹ God knew them before he made the world, and he decided that they would be like his Son so that Jesus would be the firstborn of many brothers.

*Romans 8:26–29*

4. We know from this Scripture that God's overall will is that his people be like Jesus. How does knowing this help us discern God's will with specific decisions in our lives?

_____

_____

_____

_____

_____

_____

5. What seems to stand in the way of knowing God's will?

_____

_____

_____

_____

_____

6. When you are struggling with a specific decision, how does it help you to know that the Spirit of God is interpreting your prayers?

_____

_____

_____

_____

# More from the Word

³⁵ Then Jesus said, "I am the bread that gives life. Whoever comes to me will never be hungry, and whoever believes in me will never be thirsty. ³⁶ But as I told you before, you have seen me and still don't believe. ³⁷ The Father gives me my people. Every one of them will come to me, and I will always accept them. ³⁸ I came down from heaven to do what God wants me to do, not what I want to do. ³⁹ Here is what the One who sent me wants me to do: I must not lose even one whom God gave me, but I must raise them all on the last day. ⁴⁰ Those who see the Son and believe in him have eternal life, and I will raise them on the last day. This is what my Father wants."

*John 6:35-40*

7. From what you know about Jesus' life, what kinds of habits or lifestyle choices kept him clear-minded and prepared to know God's will?

_____

_____

_____

_____

8. How can we, through our lifestyle and spiritual disciplines, put ourselves in the best frame of mind to discover God's will?

_____

_____

_____

_____

_____

9. How would you state your understanding of God's will for believers' lives?

_____

_____

_____

_____ 55

_____

# My Reflections

"God is not the God of confusion, and wherever he sees sincere seekers with confused hearts, you can bet your sweet December that he will do whatever it takes to help them see his will.

"The key to knowing God's heart is having a relationship with him . . . Walk with him long enough, and you come to know his heart. When you spend time with him in his Study, you see his passion. Welcome him to enter the gateway of your soul, and you'll perceive his will . . . and to discover his will is to access a world like none you've ever seen." —Max

# Journal

**God, I need to know your will about . . .**

_____

_____

_____

_____

_____

_____

_____

_____

_____

_____

_____

_____

_____

_____

_____

_____

# For Further Study

To study more about God's will read Jeremiah 29:11–13; John 6:40; Romans 12:1–2; 1 Thessalonians 4:3–7; 1 Peter 2:15–17; 1 Peter 3:15–19.

# Additional Questions

10. In what ways is God's will a mystery?

_____

_____

_____

_____

_____

_____

_____

11. How is figuring out God's will like figuring out what a spouse or friend wants?

_____

_____

_____

_____

_____

_____

_____

**12.** How does understanding God's will differ from understanding the will of a spouse or friend?

_____

_____

_____

_____

_____

_____

## Additional Thoughts

_____

_____

_____

_____

_____

_____

_____

_____

_____

_____

_____

# The Furnace

*"In the Great House of God there is a furnace. This furnace affects the whole house, and your prayers fuel the furnace. Your intercession is coal on the fire. Your pleadings are kindling to the flames. The furnace is sturdy, the vents are ready; all that is needed is your prayer."*
— *Max Lucado*

61

1. In what ways is prayer like a flame?

_____

_____

_____

_____

_____

_____

_____

_____

# A Moment with Max

Max shares these insights with us in his book *The Great House of God*.

You and I live in a loud world. To get someone's attention is no easy task. He must be willing to set everything aside to listen; turn down the radio, turn away from the monitor, turn the corner of the page and set down the book. When someone is willing to silence everything else so he can hear us clearly, it is a privilege. A rare privilege, indeed.

You can talk to God because God listens. Your voice matters in heaven. He takes you very seriously. When you enter his presence, the attendants turn to you to hear your voice. No need to fear that you will be ignored. Even if you stammer or stumble, even if what you have to say impresses no one, it impresses God, and he listens. He listens to the painful plea of the elderly in the rest home. He listens to the gruff confession of the death-row inmate. When the alcoholic begs for mercy, when the spouse seeks guidance, when the businessman steps off the street into the chapel, God listens.

Intently. Carefully. The prayers are honored as precious jewels . . . your words do not stop until they reach the very throne of God.

2. How do you respond to the statement, "Your voice matters in heaven"?

62

_____

_____

_____

_____

_____

3. What does the act of prayer accomplish in your life?

_____

_____

_____

_____

_____

_____

# A Message from the Word

¹ I cry out to the Lord;
    I pray to the Lord for mercy.
² I pour out my problems to him;
    I tell him my troubles.
³ When I am afraid,
    you, Lord, know the way out.
In the path where I walk,
    a trap is hidden for me.
⁴ Look around me and see.
    No one cares about me.
I have no place of safety;
    no one cares if I live.
⁵ Lord, I cry out to you.
    I say, "You are my protection.
       You are all I want in this life."
⁶ Listen to my cry,
    because I am helpless.
Save me from those who are chasing me,
    because they are too strong for me.
⁷ Free me from my prison,
    and then I will praise your name.
Then good people will surround me,
    because you have taken care of me.

*Psalm 142:1-7*

63

*Rev. 8:4 3.* [handwritten annotation]

4. How is praying to God like talking with a friend?

_____

_____

_____

_____

_____

5. In what ways does praying to God benefit you much differently than talking with a friend?

_____

_____

_____

_____

_____

6. What usually prompts you to pray?

_____

_____

_____

_____

# More from the Word

[13] Anyone who is having troubles should pray. Anyone who is happy should sing praises. [14] Anyone who is sick should call the church's elders. They should pray for and pour oil on the person in the name of the Lord. [15] And the prayer that is said with faith will make the sick person well; the Lord will heal that person. And if the person has sinned, the sins will be forgiven. [16] Confess your sins to each other and pray for each other so God can heal you. When a believing person prays, great things happen. [17] Elijah was a human being just like us. He prayed that it would not rain, and it did not rain on the land for three and a half years! [18] Then Elijah prayed again, and the rain came down from the sky, and the land produced crops again.

*James 5:13–18*

7. How does your faith affect your prayers?

_____

_____

_____

_____

_____

8. Why don't we pray even though we believe that praying will make a difference?

_____

_____

_____

_____

65

_____

_____

9. Max compares prayer to a furnace. To what would you compare prayer?

_____

_____

_____

_____

_____

_____

# My Reflections

"You have access to God's furnace. Your prayers move God to change the world. You may not understand the mystery of prayer. You don't need to. But this much is clear: Actions in heaven begin when someone prays on earth. What an amazing thought!" —Max

# Journal

God, these are the things I need to say and *really* need someone to listen to . . .

_____

_____

_____

_____

_____

_____

_____

_____

_____

_____

_____

_____

# For Further Study

To study more about prayer read Romans 12:12; Ephesians 6:18; Philippians 4:6; Colossians 4:2; 1 Thessalonians 5:17; 1 Timothy 2:8; 1 Peter 3:12; 1 Peter 4:7.

# Additional Questions

10. What do you find difficult to understand about prayer?

_____

_____

_____

_____

_____

11. If you could ask God something directly about prayer, what would it be?

_____

_____

_____

_____

_____

**12.** If there was a how-to manual about prayer, what would be the first direction?

_____

_____

_____

_____

_____

_____

## Additional Thoughts

_____ 69

_____

_____

_____

_____

_____

_____

_____

_____

_____

_____

_____

# The Kitchen

*"Whether yours was a campfire in the jungle or a culinary castle in Manhattan, you learned early that in this room your basic needs were supplied. A garage is optional. A living room is negotiable. An office is a luxury. But a kitchen? Absolutely essential. Every house has one. Even the Great House of God."*

—*Max Lucado*

71

1. What place did your kitchen hold in the home in which you grew up?

_____

_____

_____

_____

_____

_____

_____

# A Moment with Max

Max shares these insights with us in his book *The Great House of God*.

The kitchen in God's house is no restaurant. It's not owned by a stranger; it's run by your Father. It's not a place to visit and leave; it's a place to linger and chat. It's not open one hour and closed the next; the kitchen is ever available. You don't eat and then pay; you eat and say thanks. But perhaps the most important difference between a kitchen and a restaurant is the menu. A kitchen doesn't have one.

God's kitchen doesn't need one. Things may be different in your house, but in the house of God, the one who provides the food is the one who prepares the meal. We don't swagger into his presence and demand delicacies. Nor do we sit outside the door and hope for crumbs. We simply take our place at the table and gladly trust him to "Give us this day our daily bread."

What a statement of trust! Whatever you want me to have is all I want.

2. In what ways might our lives be different if God let us order his provision from a menu?

_____

_____

_____

_____

_____

3. What, if any, circumstances in your life have convinced you that God gives his people what they need whether they realize it at the time or not?

_____

_____

_____

_____

_____

# A Message from the Word

[1] The Lord is my shepherd;
   I have everything I need.
[2] He lets me rest in green pastures.
   He leads me to calm water.
[3] He gives me new strength.
   He leads me on paths that are right
      for the good of his name.
[4] Even if I walk through a very dark valley,
   I will not be afraid,
 because you are with me.
   Your rod and your walking stick comfort me.
[5] You prepare a meal for me
   in front of my enemies.
 You pour oil on my head;
   you fill my cup to overflowing.
[6] Surely your goodness and love will be with me
   all my life,
      and I will live in the house of the Lord forever.

*Psalm 23:1-6*     73

4. When did God meet a specific need for you?

_____

_____

_____

_____

_____

5. Besides food and water, what do you consider to be your basic needs?

_____

_____

_____

_____

6. How do you determine the difference between what you need from God (and therefore can expect him to give) and what you want from God?

_____

_____

_____

_____

_____

# More from the Word

[7] "I ask two things from you, Lord.
   Don't refuse me before I die.
[8] Keep me from lying and being dishonest.
   And don't make me either rich or poor;
      just give me enough food for each day.
[9] If I have too much, I might reject you
   and say, 'I don't know the Lord.'
   If I am poor, I might steal
      and disgrace the name of my God.

*Proverbs 30:7-9*

7. What are the dangers of being too rich or too poor?

_____

_____

_____

_____

_____

8. What convinces you that you can trust God to give you what you need?

_____

_____

_____

_____

_____

9. How does trusting God to give you what you need affect the way you face life's circumstances?

_____

_____

_____

_____

_____

_____

## My Reflections

"Some days the plate runs over . . . And then there are those days when, well, when we have to eat our broccoli.

"The next time your plate has more broccoli than apple pie, remember who prepared the meal. And the next time your plate has a portion you find hard to swallow, talk to God about it." —Max

# Journal

These are the parts of my life I find hard to swallow:

_____

_____

_____

_____

_____

_____

_____

_____

_____

_____

_____

_____

_____

_____

_____

_____

_____

# For Further Study

To study more about God's provision read 1 Chronicles 29:14; Psalm 37:3-4; Philippians 4:12; Hebrews 13:20-21.

# Additional Questions

10. What circumstances of life are like apple pie on your plate?

_____

_____

_____

_____

_____

_____

11. What circumstances of life are like broccoli on your plate?

_____

_____

_____

_____

_____

_____

12. What circumstances of life are like an empty plate to you?

_____

_____

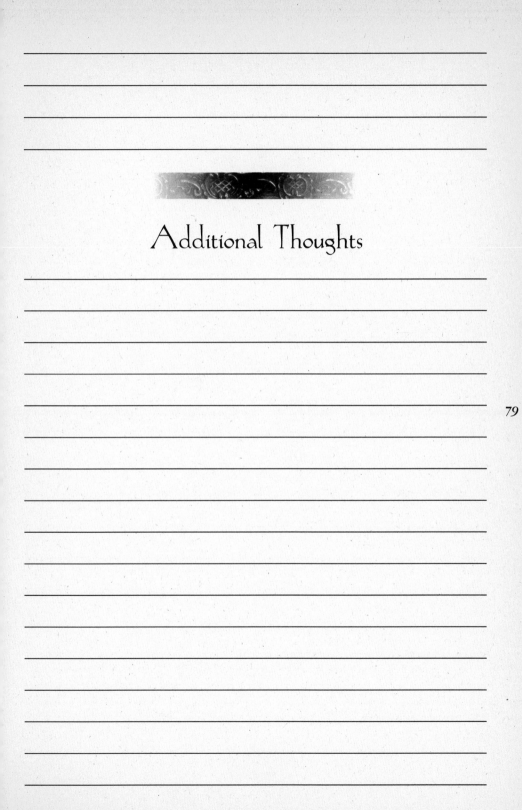

# Additional Thoughts

79

# The Roof

*"What do you do if you don't have any money? What do you do if you have nothing to deposit but an honest apology and good intentions? You pray that some wealthy soul will make a huge deposit in your account. If you're talking about your financial debt, that's not likely to happen. If you're talking about your spiritual debt, however, it already has. Your Father has covered your shortfall. In God's house you are covered by the roof of his grace." —Max Lucado*

1. How is sinfulness like a debt?

_____

_____

_____

_____

# A Moment with Max

Max shares these insights with us in his book *The Great House of God.*

Debt. The Greek word for debt has no mystery. It simply means "to owe someone something." If to be in debt is to owe someone something, isn't it appropriate for us [to] speak of debt in our prayer, for aren't we all in debt to God?

Aren't we in God's debt when we disobey his commands? He tells us to go south and we go north. He tells us to turn right and we turn left . . . Instead of seeking *his* will, we seek *our* will.

Aren't we in God's debt when we disregard him? He makes the universe and we applaud science. He heals the sick and we applaud medicine. He grants beauty and we credit Mother Nature. He gives us possessions and we salute human ingenuity.

"You mean every time I do one of these things, I'm writing a check on my heavenly bank account?"

That's exactly what I'm saying. I'm also saying that if Christ had not covered us with his grace, each of us would be overdrawn on that account. When it comes to goodness we would have insufficient funds. Inadequate holiness. God requires a certain balance of virtue in our account, and it's more than any of us has alone. Our holiness account shows insufficient funds, and only the holy will see the Lord; what can we do?

82

2. What does it feel like to have spiritual insufficient funds?

_____

_____

_____

_____

3. How does God replenish your account with him?

_____

_____

_____

_____

# A Message from the Word

[17] If anyone belongs to Christ, there is a new creation. The old things have gone; everything is made new! [18] All this is from God. Through Christ, God made peace between us and himself, and God gave us the work of telling everyone about the peace we can have with him. [19] God was in Christ, making peace between the world and himself. In Christ, God did not hold the world guilty of its sins. And he gave us this message of peace. [20] So we have been sent to speak for Christ. It is as if God is calling to you through us. We speak for Christ when we beg you to be at peace with God. [21] Christ had no sin, but God made him become sin so that in Christ we could become right with God.

[1] We are workers together with God, so we beg you: Do not let the grace that you received from God be for nothing. [2] God says,

"At the right time I heard your prayers.
On the day of salvation I helped you."

I tell you that the "right time" is now, and the "day of salvation" is now.

*2 Corinthians 5:17—6:2*

83

4. How is a person's reconciliation by God similar to the reconciliation of a bank account?

_____

_____

_____

_____

_____

5. Banks send monthly statements that review a person's financial situation. What would be the equivalent in one's spiritual account?

_____

_____

_____

_____

_____

6. What happens in the life of one who has a healthy, reconciled spiritual account with God?

_____

_____

_____

_____

# More from the Word

84 [1] Since we have been made right with God by our faith, we have peace with God. This happened through our Lord Jesus Christ, [2] who has brought us into that blessing of God's grace that we now enjoy. And we are happy because of the hope we have of sharing God's glory. [3] We also have joy with our troubles, because we know that these troubles produce patience. [4] And patience produces character, and character produces hope. [5] And this hope will never disappoint us, because God has poured out his love to fill our hearts. He gave us his love through the Holy Spirit, whom God has given to us.

[6] When we were unable to help ourselves, at the moment of our need, Christ died for us, although we were living against God.

*Romans 5:1-6*

7. How is being justified before God like being reconciled to him?

_____

_____

_____

8. In what ways is our character affected by how clean we keep our account before God?

_____

_____

_____

_____

_____

9. With what currency does God replenish our spiritual bank account?

_____

_____

_____

_____

# My Reflections

"Picture, if you will, a blank check. The amount of the check is 'sufficient grace.' The signer of the check is Jesus. The only blank line is for the payee. That part is for you. May I urge you to spend a few moments with your Savior receiving this check? Reflect on the work of his grace. Look toward the roof. Its beams are from Calvary and the nails once held a Savior to the cross. His sacrifice was for you.

"Whether for the first time or the thousandth, let him hear you whisper, 'Forgive us our debts.' And let him answer your prayer as you imagine writing your name on the check." —Max

# Journal

**When I think about standing clean and guilt-free before God, I want to . . .**

_____

_____

_____

_____

_____

_____

_____

_____

_____

_____

_____

_____

_____

_____

_____

_____

_____

# For Further Study

To study more about God's grace read Isaiah 53:5; Romans 4:5; 5:15; 8:33; Galatians 3:13; Ephesians 2:4–10; 1 Corinthians 15:10; 2 Corinthians 8:9; 1 Peter 3:18.

# Additional Questions

10. What does it feel like to be in deep debt?

_____

_____

_____

_____

_____

_____

_____

11. When did you owe someone so much you didn't know how you'd pay it? What happened?

_____

_____

_____

_____

_____

_____

**12. What does it feel like to make that last payment that clears a debt?**

_____

_____

_____

_____

_____

_____

## Additional Thoughts

_____

_____

89

_____

_____

_____

_____

_____

_____

_____

_____

_____

_____

_____

# The Hallway

*"**W**hat are you going to do with those in your debt? People in your past have dipped their hands in your purse and taken what was yours. What are you going to do? Few questions are more important. Dealing with debt is at the heart of your happiness. It's also at the heart of the Lord's prayer."* —Max Lucado

91

1. Think of a time when you needed to forgive someone. What are the challenges to forgiveness?

_____

_____

_____

_____

_____

_____

_____

# A Moment with Max

Max shares these insights with us in his book *The Great House of God*.

Through the center of the Great House of God runs a large hallway. You can't get from one room to another without using it . . . You can't go anywhere without walking the hallways. And you can't walk the hallway without bumping into people.

Jesus does not question the reality of your wounds. He does not doubt that you have been sinned against. The issue is not the *existence* of pain, the issue is the *treatment* of pain. What are you going to do with your debts?

"Forgive us our debts as we have forgiven our debtors."

"Treat me as I treat my neighbor." Are you aware that this is what you are saying to your Father? Give me what I give them. Grant me the same peace I grant others. Let me enjoy the same tolerance I offer. God will treat you the way you treat others.

2. In our daily interactions, what keeps us from showing mercy like God has shown us?

_____

_____

_____

_____

_____

3. Today, what would be the equivalent of "an eye for an eye and a tooth for a tooth"?

_____

_____

_____

_____

_____

_____

# A Message from the Word

38 "You have heard that it was said, 'An eye for an eye, and a tooth for a tooth.' 39 But I tell you, don't stand up against an evil person. If someone slaps you on the right cheek, turn to him the other cheek also. 40 If someone wants to sue you in court and take your shirt, let him have your coat also. 41 If someone forces you to go with him one mile, go with him two miles. 42 If a person asks you for something, give it to him. Don't refuse to give to someone who wants to borrow from you.

43. "You have heard that it was said, 'Love your neighbor and hate your enemies.' 44 But I say to you, love your enemies. Pray for those who hurt you. 45 If you do this, you will be true children of your Father in heaven. He causes the sun to rise on good people and on evil people, and he sends rain to those who do right and to those who do wrong. 46 If you love only the people who love you, you will get no reward. Even the tax collectors do that. 47 And if you are nice only to your friends, you are no better than other people. Even those who don't know God are nice to their friends. 48 So you must be perfect, just as your Father in heaven is perfect.

*Matthew 5:38-48*

93

4. What was the purpose of Jesus' command to love people more than they love us?

_____

_____

_____

_____

_____

5. How do you balance having Jesus' kind of generosity with taking care of yourself and your belongings?

_____

_____

_____

_____

_____

6. What are the benefits of living your life with Jesus' "give until it hurts" mentality?

_____

_____

_____

_____

_____

# More from the Word

[1] "Don't judge other people, or you will be judged. [2] You will be judged in the same way that you judge others, and the amount you give to others will be given to you.

[3] "Why do you notice the little piece of dust in your friend's eye, but you don't notice the big piece of wood in your own eye? [4] How can you say to your friend, 'Let me take that little piece of dust out of your eye'? Look at yourself! You still have that big piece of wood in your own eye. [5] You hypocrite! First, take the wood out of your own eye. Then you will see clearly to take the dust out of your friend's eye.

*Matthew 7:1-5*

7. What does it mean to judge someone?

_____

_____

_____

_____

_____

8. What is a current illustration of pointing out the speck in someone else's eye and ignoring the plank in your own eye?

_____

_____

_____

_____

_____

9. When have you seen individuals being judged the way they have, themselves, judged?

_____

_____

_____

_____

_____

_____

# My Reflections

"Could it be God is giving you exactly what you're giving someone else?

"Would you like some peace? Then quit giving your neighbor such a hassle. Want to enjoy God's generosity? Then let others enjoy yours. Would you like assurance that God forgives you? I think you know what you need to do." —Max

# Journal

**Where do I need to spread some mercy?**

# For Further Study

To study more about forgiveness read Psalm 32:1; Matthew 6:12; Matthew 6:14–15; Matthew 18:23–35; Luke 6:37–38; Luke 7:36–48; Romans 14:9–10.

# Additional Questions

10. What is the role of mercy in the life of a Christian?

_____

_____

_____

_____

_____

_____

11. What is the most forgiving act you've ever witnessed?

_____

_____

_____

_____

_____

_____

_____

12. What is the greatest lack of mercy or forgiveness you've ever seen?

_____

_____

_____

_____

_____

_____

## Additional Thoughts

_____

_____

_____

_____

_____

_____

_____

_____

_____

_____

_____

_____

# The Walls

*"Over and over the Bible makes it clear who really runs the earth. Satan may strut and prance, but it's God who calls the shots."*
— *Max Lucado*

101

1. What does it mean to your everyday life that God is sovereign (or in charge)?

_____

_____

_____

_____

_____

_____

_____

_____

# A Moment with Max

Max shares these insights with us in his book *The Great House of God.*

The next-to-last phrase in the Lord's prayer is a petition for protection from Satan: "And lead us not into temptation, but deliver us from the evil one."

Is such a prayer necessary? Would God ever lead us into temptation? These words trouble the most sophisticated theologian.

The phrase is best understood with this simple illustration. Imagine a father and son walking down an icy street. The father cautions the boy to be careful, but the boy is too excited to slow down. He hits the first patch of ice. Up go the feet and down plops the bottom. Dad comes along and helps him to his feet. The boy apologizes for disregarding the warning and then, tightly holding his father's big hand, he asks, "Keep me from the slippery spots. Don't let me fall again."

The Father is so willing to comply. "The steps of the godly are directed by the Lord. He delights in every detail of their lives. Though they stumble, they will not fall, for the Lord holds them by the hand" (Psalm 37:23-24 TLB).

2. What does it feel like to be tempted to do something wrong?

_____

_____

_____

_____

_____

3. What distracts people from turning to God when they are tempted?

_____

_____

_____

_____

_____

_____

_____

# A Message from the Word

[1] Brothers and sisters, if someone in your group does something wrong, you who are spiritual should go to that person and gently help make him right again. But be careful, because you might be tempted to sin, too. [2] By helping each other with your troubles, you truly obey the law of Christ. [3] If anyone thinks he is important when he really is not, he is only fooling himself. [4] Each person should judge his own actions and not compare himself with others. Then he can be proud for what he himself has done. [5] Each person must be responsible for himself.

[6] Anyone who is learning the teaching of God should share all the good things he has with his teacher.

[7] Do not be fooled: You cannot cheat God. People harvest only what they plant. [8] If they plant to satisfy their sinful selves, their sinful selves will bring them ruin. But if they plant to please the Spirit, they will receive eternal life from the Spirit.

*Galatians 6:1-8*

4. What is your definition of temptation?

_____

_____

_____

_____

_____

5. In what ways can we help each other avoid evil?

_____

_____

_____

_____

_____

6. How does Jesus' example help deliver us from evil?

_____

_____

_____

_____

_____

_____

# More from the Word

[14] Since we have a great high priest, Jesus the Son of God, who has gone into heaven, let us hold on to the faith we have. [15] For our high priest is able to understand our weaknesses. When he lived on earth, he was tempted in every way that we are, but he did not sin. [16] Let us, then, feel very sure that we can come before God's throne where there is grace. There we can receive mercy and grace to help us when we need it.

*Hebrews 4:14–16*

7. How is it comforting or helpful to realize that Christ knows your struggle with temptation?

_____

_____

_____

_____

_____

_____

8. What keeps you from approaching God's throne of grace with confidence?

_____

_____

_____

_____

_____

_____

9. How would you describe the difference between being tempted by Satan to do evil things and being tempted by circumstances and your own sinful nature to do evil things?

_____

_____

_____

_____

_____

_____

# My Reflections

"Such is the heart of this petition. It's a tender request of a child to a father. The last few slips have taught us—the walk is too treacherous to make alone. So we place our small hand in his large one and say, 'Please, *Abba*, keep me from evil.'" —Max

# Journal

**What evil do I fear this week, either within me or around me?**

_____

_____

_____

_____

_____

_____

_____

_____

_____

_____

_____

_____

_____

_____

_____

_____

_____

# For Further Study

To study more about temptation read Matthew 4:1-11; Romans 1:18-27; 1 Corinthians 10:7-13; 2 Corinthians 12:7-10; James 1:12-17.

# Additional Questions

10. What temptations pose the greatest challenge to you?

_____

_____

_____

_____

_____

_____

_____

11. What strategies do people commonly use to say no to everyday temptations?

_____

_____

_____

_____

_____

_____

_____

12. What kind of evils do you see around you everyday?

_____

_____

_____

_____

_____

_____

_____

## Additional Thoughts

_____

_____

_____

_____

_____

_____

_____

_____

_____

_____

_____

_____

# The Chapel Revisited

*"There are certain mountains we were never made to climb. Ascend them and you'll end up bruised and embarrassed. Stay away from them and you'll sidestep a lot of stress. These mountains are described in the final phrase of the Lord's Prayer, 'Thine is the kingdom and the power and the glory forever. Amen.'"*
—*Max Lucado*

111

1. How do you decide which mountains in life are yours to climb and which ones are God's?

_____

_____

_____

_____

_____

_____

# A Moment with Max

Max shares these insights with us in his book *The Great House of God*.

Our Lord's prayer has given us a blueprint for the Great House of God ...
And now, having seen every room and explored each corner, we have one
final stop ... we return to the chapel. We return to the room of worship.
The chapel, remember, is where we stand before God and confess,
"Hallowed be thy name."

The chapel is the only room in the house of God we visit twice. It's not
hard to see why. It does us twice as much good to think about God as it
does to think about anyone or anything else. God wants us to begin and
end our prayers thinking of him. Jesus is urging us to look at the peak more
than we look at the trail. The more we focus up there, the more inspired we
are down here.

"Thine is the kingdom and the power and the glory forever." What protection this final phrase affords.

As you confess that God is in charge, you admit that you aren't. As you
proclaim that God has power, you admit that you don't. And as you give
God all the applause, there is none left to dizzy your brain.

112

2. What changes about the way you look at your circumstances when you
are deliberately aware of God's control over life?

_____

_____

_____

_____

_____

3. How does recognizing God's sovereignty affect your worship?

_____

_____

_____

_____

_____

# A Message from the Word

³ Glorify the Lord with me,
   and let us praise his name together.
⁴ I asked the Lord for help, and he answered me.
   He saved me from all that I feared.
⁵ Those who go to him for help are happy,
   and they are never disgraced.
⁶ This poor man called, and the Lord heard him
   and saved him from all his troubles.
⁷ The angel of the Lord camps around those who fear God,
   and he saves them.
⁸ Examine and see how good the Lord is.
   Happy is the person who trusts him.
⁹ You who belong to the Lord, fear him!
   Those who fear him will have everything they need.
¹⁰ Even lions may get weak and hungry,
   but those who look to the Lord will have every good thing.

*Psalm 34:3-10*

4. How do you describe the power of God?

_____

_____

_____

_____

_____

5. This psalm lists many images of God's greatness. What is your most vivid image of God's greatness?

_____

_____

_____

6. If you recognize God's greatness, why are you often amazed when he does something great?

_____

_____

_____

_____

_____

# More from the Word

[37] A very strong wind came up on the lake. The waves came over the sides and into the boat so that it was already full of water. [38] Jesus was at the back of the boat, sleeping with his head on a cushion. His followers woke him and said, "Teacher, don't you care that we are drowning!"

[39] Jesus stood up and commanded the wind and said to the waves, "Quiet! Be still!" Then the wind stopped, and it became completely calm.

[40] Jesus said to his followers, "Why are you afraid? Do you still have no faith?"

[41] The followers were very afraid and asked each other, "Who is this? Even the wind and the waves obey him!"

*Mark 4:37-41*

7. What is your explanation for how the disciples could live every day with Jesus as he worked miracles and yet be surprised when he controlled nature?

_____

_____

_____

_____

_____

8. What can we learn from Jesus' rebuke of the disciples?

_____

_____

_____

_____

9. Why is it appropriate to end the Lord's Prayer by re-affirming God's sovereignty?

_____

_____

_____

_____

# My Reflections

"The Lord's prayer is a floor plan of the house of God: a step-by-step description of how God meets our needs when we dwell in him. Everything that occurs in a healthy house is described in this prayer.

" 'Then why don't more people feel protected, forgiven, or instructed?'

"My answer is as simple as the question is direct. Most have not learned to dwell in the house. Oh we visit it. We stop in for the day or even drop by for a meal. But abide here? This is God's desire." —Max

# Journal

**How can I dwell more consistently in God's house?**

# For Further Study

To study more about God's power and sovereignty read Psalm 68:34-35; 77:14-15; Mark 1:27-28; Ephesians 1:21-23; Colossians 3:1-2; 1 John 4:4.

# Additional Questions

10. What is the kingdom of God like?

_____

_____

_____

_____

_____

_____

11. What distracts people from God's presence?

_____

_____

_____

_____

_____

_____

_____

12. What calls people back home to God's house when they have wandered away?

_____

_____

_____

_____

_____

_____

## Additional Thoughts

_____

_____

_____

_____

_____

_____

_____

_____

_____

_____

_____

_____

_____